Beneath the Surface Mining in Emalahleni Local Community

Hemilton Thabo Mtsweni

Published by Hemilton Thabo Mtsweni, 2024.

While every precaution has been taken in the preparation of this book, the publisher assumes no responsibility for errors or omissions, or for damages resulting from the use of the information contained herein.

BENEATH THE SURFACE MINING IN EMALAHLENI LOCAL COMMUNITY

First edition. March 23, 2024.

Copyright © 2024 Hemilton Thabo Mtsweni.

ISBN: 979-8224638635

Written by Hemilton Thabo Mtsweni.

Also by Hemilton Thabo Mtsweni

Beneath the Surface Mining in Emalahleni Local Community

Table of Contents

Dedication

We, the undersigned representatives of HTN Publishers, hereby declare our commitment to excellence, integrity, and innovation in the field of publishing. As a subsidiary of HTN Nsimbiken Holdings, we recognize our responsibility to uphold the values and principles of our parent company while striving to meet the unique needs and expectations of our readers, authors, and stakeholders.

1. Commitment to Quality: We pledge to produce and disseminate content of the highest quality across various genres and formats, enriching the lives of our audience and contributing to the cultural and intellectual enrichment of society. 2. Ethical Conduct: We affirm our dedication to conducting our business with integrity, transparency, and honesty. We will adhere to ethical standards in all aspects of our operations, ensuring fairness and trustworthiness in our interactions with authors, partners, and the public. 3. Innovation and Adaptability: Recognizing the rapidly evolving nature of the publishing industry, we commit to embracing innovation and staying at the forefront of technological advancements. We will explore new avenues for content delivery, harnessing digital platforms and emerging technologies to enhance accessibility and engagement. 4. Diversity and Inclusivity: We embrace diversity in all its forms and are committed to fostering an inclusive publishing environment. We will actively seek out and promote diverse voices, perspectives, and experiences, reflecting the richness and complexity of the human story. 5. Community Engagement: We recognize the importance of engaging with our community of readers, authors, and partners. We will actively seek feedback, listen to concerns, and foster meaningful dialogue to better serve and connect with our audience. 6. Environmental Responsibility: We acknowledge our responsibility to minimize our environmental impact and promote sustainability in our publishing practices. We will strive to reduce waste, conserve resources, and implement eco-friendly initiatives wherever possible.

By affixing our signatures below, we affirm our dedication to upholding the principles outlined in this declaration and to advancing the mission and vision of HTN Publishers.

Chapter 1: Introduction to Emalahleni

Overview of Emalahleni's history, geography, and demographics.

Emalahleni, also known as Witbank, is a city located in the Mpumalanga province of South Africa. Historically, it was established in the late 19th century as a coal mining town. The name "Emalahleni" means "place of coal" in Zulu.

Geographically, Emalahleni is situated in the Highveld region, characterised by its rolling grasslands and coal reserves. It lies approximately 110 kilometres east of Johannesburg.Demographically, Emalahleni has a diverse population consisting of various ethnic groups, including Zulu, Ndebele, Sotho, and others. Due to its history as a mining town, it has attracted people from different parts of South Africa seeking employment in the coal mines. This has contributed to its multicultural makeup.Economically, Emalahleni is heavily reliant on the coal mining industry, with several coal mines operating in the area. Additionally, it serves as a commercial hub for the surrounding agricultural and industrial activities.Overall, Emalahleni's history, geography, and demographics are closely intertwined with its role as a coal mining centre and its significance in the regional economy of Mpumalanga.

Introduction to the significance of mining in the region.

The significance of mining in Emalahleni, also known as Witbank, is deeply rooted in the city's history, economy, and social fabric.

- **Historical Importance:** Emalahleni's emergence as a prominent mining centre dates back to the late 19th century when coal deposits were discovered in the area. The exploitation of these coal reserves fuelled the city's growth and development, shaping its identity as a mining town.

- **Economic Backbone:** Mining, particularly coal mining, remains the backbone of Emalahleni's economy. The city is home to numerous coal mines, which not only provide employment opportunities for local residents but also contribute significantly to the regional and national economies through exports and revenue generation.

- **Employment Opportunities:** The mining industry in Emalahleni is a major employer, offering jobs to a significant portion of the local population. This employment extends beyond the mines themselves to various support industries and service sectors, creating a multiplier effect on the economy.

- **Infrastructure Development:** The presence of mining activities has spurred infrastructure development in Emalahleni, including transportation networks, housing developments, and amenities to support the mining workforce and their families.

- **Environmental and Social Challenges:** Despite its economic benefits, mining in Emalahleni also presents environmental and social challenges. Issues such as air and water pollution, land degradation, and health concerns for miners and nearby communities are significant considerations that need to be addressed sustainably.

In summary, the significance of mining in Emalahleni is multifaceted, encompassing its historical roots, economic importance, employment opportunities, infrastructure development, and associated challenges. It remains a central pillar of the city's identity and continues to shape its trajectory into the future.

Chapter 2: Geological Foundations

Emalahleni's geological story begins with the Karoo Supergroup, a vast sedimentary sequence that spans across Southern Africa. Within the Karoo Supergroup, the Ecca Group holds paramount importance for coal formation. The Ecca Group, deposited during the Permian period approximately 300 to 250 million years ago, comprises a diverse array of sedimentary rocks, including sandstones, shales, and crucially, coal seams.

The formation of coal within the Ecca Group is intricately linked to the paleo environmental conditions prevalent during the Permian period. At that time, the Emalahleni region experienced dynamic changes in sea levels and climatic fluctuations. These environmental shifts created extensive swampy landscapes and marshlands, providing the ideal setting for the accumulation of organic matter.

The organic-rich sediments primarily originated from plant material thriving in these swampy environments. As plants died and accumulated in stagnant waterlogged conditions, they underwent partial decomposition under anaerobic conditions, leading to the formation of peat. Over time, successive layers of sediment buried the peat, subjecting it to increasing pressure and temperature.

Tectonic activity further influenced the burial and preservation of these organic-rich sediments. As the Earth's crust underwent tectonic movements, sedimentation processes continued to deposit layers of sediment atop the organic material. The compaction and heating resulting from the overlying sediment layers initiated a process known as diagenesis, wherein the peat gradually transformed into coal.

The type and quality of coal formed depended on various factors, including the composition of the original plant material, the depth of burial, and the duration of heat and pressure exposure. In the case of Emalahleni, the coal deposits predominantly consist of bituminous coal, prized for its high energy content and suitability for industrial applications.

The culmination of these geological processes over millions of years has endowed Emalahleni with extensive coal reserves, making it a cornerstone of South Africa's coal mining industry. The economic significance of these coal deposits extends beyond the city, contributing significantly to the regional and national economies.

However, alongside the economic prosperity brought about by coal mining, Emalahleni also grapples with environmental and social challenges. The extraction and utilisation of coal have environmental implications, including air and water pollution, land degradation, and greenhouse gas emissions. Additionally, the mining industry's reliance on a transient labor force has social repercussions on local communities and labourers.

Emalahleni's status as a hub for coal mining is intricately intertwined with its geological heritage. The geological formations of the Karoo Supergroup, particularly the Ecca Group, provided the fertile grounds for the formation and preservation of coal over geological time scales. Understanding these geological processes not only sheds light on Emalahleni's past but also informs discussions about its sustainable future amidst the challenges posed by coal mining.

The Witbank Coalfields, nestled in the heart of Mpumalanga province, South Africa, stand as a testament to the nation's rich mineral wealth. Renowned for their extensive coal reserves and high-quality output, these coalfields have played a pivotal role in shaping the region's economic landscape and contributing to the nation's energy security. This essay provides an in-depth exploration of the Witbank Coalfields, delving into their geological significance, economic impact, environmental considerations, and future prospects.

Economic Impact:

The economic significance of the Witbank Coalfields cannot be overstated. Coal mining operations in the region have been a driving force behind local and regional economic development for well over a century. The employment opportunities generated by the coal mining industry provide livelihoods for thousands of individuals, supporting families and communities across the region. Moreover, the revenue generated from coal exports contributes to South Africa's foreign exchange earnings, bolstering the nation's economy and global competitiveness.

Environmental Considerations:

While the Witbank Coalfields have been a source of economic prosperity, they have also presented environmental challenges that require careful management and mitigation. Coal mining activities, particularly opencast mining, can have adverse impacts on air and water quality, soil stability, and biodiversity. Efforts to minimise these impacts through environmental management practices, rehabilitation of mined areas, and adoption of cleaner technologies are essential for ensuring sustainable coal mining practices in the region.

Future Prospects:

Looking ahead, the Witbank Coalfields continue to hold promise for the future, albeit within the context of shifting energy dynamics and environmental imperatives. As the world transitions towards cleaner and more sustainable energy sources, the coal mining industry in the region may need to adapt and diversify. This could involve exploring opportunities for coal benefaction, value-added processing, and reclamation of abandoned mine sites for alternative land uses. Additionally, investment in renewable energy projects and green technologies could help mitigate the environmental footprint of coal mining activities while promoting economic diversification and job creation.

In conclusion, the Witbank Coalfields stand as a cornerstone of South Africa's mining industry, embodying the nation's rich mineral heritage and economic potential. As stewards of this precious resource, it is imperative that we strike a balance between harnessing the economic benefits of coal mining and safeguarding the environment for future generations. Through responsible management, innovation, and strategic planning, the Witbank Coalfields can continue to contribute to sustainable development and prosperity in Mpumalanga and beyond.

Chapter 3: The Rise of Mining in Emalahleni

The mining industry in Emalahleni traces its origins to the late 19th century when coal was first discovered in the area. Prospectors and settlers ventured into the region in search of mineral wealth, eventually uncovering extensive coal deposits beneath the earth's surface. This discovery marked the beginning of Emalahleni's transformation into a prominent mining centre.

The early 20th century witnessed a rapid influx of miners, labourers, and entrepreneurs to Emalahleni, fuelling a period of rapid growth and urbanisation. The town burgeoned into a bustling hub of activity, with coal mines proliferating across the landscape. The coal mining boom propelled Emalahleni into the spotlight as one of South Africa's foremost coal-producing regions, driving economic prosperity and infrastructure development.

The mid-20th century saw the industrialisation and modernisation of the mining industry in Emalahleni. Mechanisation and technological advancements revolutionised coal extraction processes, leading to increased efficiency and productivity in the mines. Emalahleni became a showcase of modern mining practices, attracting investment and expertise to further enhance its mining operations.

Throughout the late 20th century, the mining industry in Emalahleni continued to expand and diversify, driven by growing domestic and international demand for coal. In addition to coal, the region also saw exploration and development of other mineral resources, such as platinum group metals (PGMs), gold, and chrome, further bolstering its economic base and contributing to job creation and revenue generation.

In the 21st century, the mining industry in Emalahleni faced increasing scrutiny and regulation regarding its social and environmental impacts. Concerns about worker safety, community development, and environmental sustainability prompted mining companies to adopt more responsible practices and engage with stakeholders to address these issues. Efforts were made to mitigate the environmental footprint of mining activities and promote sustainable development in the region.

Looking ahead, the mining industry in Emalahleni continues to play a significant role in the region's economy, albeit amidst a shifting landscape of technological innovation, environmental stewardship, and socio-economic dynamics. Emalahleni's mining sector is poised to adapt to emerging challenges and opportunities, leveraging its rich mineral endowment and expertise to navigate the complexities of the global mining industry while ensuring a sustainable and prosperous future for the municipality and its inhabitants.

The historical development of the mining industry in the Emalahleni municipality reflects a dynamic and evolving journey marked by resilience, innovation, and adaptation. From its humble beginnings as a coal mining town to its present-day prominence as a diversified mineral extraction hub, Emalahleni's mining sector remains a cornerstone of the region's economy and heritage.

The impact of mining on the local economy and communities in Emalahleni has been significant, shaping both the socio-economic landscape and the daily lives of residents. While mining has brought about economic growth and employment opportunities, it has also posed challenges and implications for local communities.

Mining has been a major driver of economic activity in Emalahleni, providing employment opportunities, generating revenue for local businesses, and contributing to government tax revenues. The direct employment in mining operations, as well as indirect employment in related sectors such as transportation, services, and manufacturing, have supported livelihoods and improved living standards for many residents.

The mining industry has spurred the development of infrastructure in Emalahleni, including roads, railways, housing, and utilities. Mining companies often invest in infrastructure projects to support their operations and accommodate the needs of their workforce. This infrastructure development has not only enhanced connectivity and accessibility but also improved the quality of life for residents.

Mining companies in Emalahleni have undertaken various social responsibility initiatives aimed at supporting local communities and fostering sustainable development. These initiatives may include investments in education, healthcare, housing, skills development, and community infrastructure. By partnering with local stakeholders and government authorities, mining companies contribute to social empowerment in the region.

Despite the economic benefits, mining activities in Emalahleni have also had environmental consequences. Open-cast mining, in particular, can result in land degradation, air and water pollution, and habitat destruction. These environmental impacts can affect the health and well-being of local communities, as well as the sustainability of natural resources and ecosystems.

The influx of migrant labourers and transient workforce associated with mining operations in Emalahleni has led to social challenges such as housing shortages, strain on public services, and cultural tensions. Additionally, communities near mining sites may experience disruptions to their traditional way of life, as well as concerns about safety, health, and land rights.

Effective engagement and participation of local communities in decision-making processes related to mining can help address social concerns and ensure that the benefits of mining are equitably distributed. By involving communities in project planning, implementation, and monitoring, mining companies can build trust, foster mutual understanding, and promote sustainable development outcomes.

The impact of mining on the local economy and communities in Emalahleni is multifaceted, encompassing both positive and negative dimensions. While mining has contributed to economic growth, infrastructure development, and social investment, it has also posed environmental challenges and social disruptions. By adopting responsible mining practices, engaging with local stakeholders, and promoting inclusive development, the mining industry in Emalahleni can strive to maximise its positive impact while mitigating its negative consequences on the region and its inhabitants.

Chapter 4: Mining Operations

In Emalahleni, various mining techniques are employed to extract coal and other minerals from the earth's crust, including both open-pit and underground mining methods. Each technique has its advantages, challenges, and environmental considerations, tailored to the geological characteristics of the deposits and the economic viability of extraction.

1. Open-Pit Mining:

Open-pit mining, also known as open-cast mining or surface mining, is a commonly used method for extracting coal and other shallow mineral deposits in Emalahleni. This technique involves the removal of overlying soil and rock to expose the coal seams or mineral deposits beneath the surface. The process typically unfolds as follows:

a. <u>Exploration</u> and Planning: Geological surveys, drilling, and sampling are conducted to identify the location, size, and quality of coal deposits. Based on this information, mining engineers develop a plan for the open-pit operation, considering factors such as ore grades, overburden thickness, and topography.

b. <u>Stripping</u>: Overburden, consisting of soil, rock, and other non-ore materials, is removed using heavy machinery such as excavators, bulldozers, and draglines. The stripped material is either stockpiled for later reclamation or used for backfilling previously mined areas.

c. <u>Extraction</u>: Once the overburden is cleared, mining equipment such as large trucks, shovels, and loaders are used to extract the coal or minerals from the exposed seams. The extracted material is then transported to processing facilities for further benefaction and refinement.

d. <u>Reclamation</u>: After mining operations are complete, the open-pit is reclaimed to restore the landscape and mitigate environmental impacts. This may involve backfilling the pit, contouring the land, and revegetating with native plant species to rehabilitate the site and promote ecosystem recovery.

Open-pit mining in Emalahleni offers advantages such as high productivity, low operating costs, and the ability to access shallow deposits. However, it also poses environmental challenges, including land degradation, habitat destruction, and visual impact on the landscape.

2. Underground Mining:

Underground mining is employed in Emalahleni to extract coal and minerals located at deeper depths below the surface. This method involves accessing the mineral deposits through vertical shafts, inclines, or adits and then extracting the ore using various underground mining techniques. The process typically unfolds as follows:

a. <u>Accessing the Deposit</u>: Vertical shafts or decline ramps are constructed to provide access to the underground workings. Tunnels and drifts are then excavated to reach the coal seams or mineralised zones.

b. <u>Development</u>: Once access is established, development work begins to prepare the underground workings for mining activities. This may involve the installation of support systems such as roof bolts, timber props, or rock bolts to stabilise the mine workings.

c. <u>Extraction</u>: Coal or mineral extraction is carried out using methods such as room and pillar mining, long wall mining, or cut-and-fill mining, depending on the geological conditions and deposit characteristics. Machinery such as continuous miners, shuttle cars, and conveyor belts are used to extract and transport the ore to the surface.

d. <u>Support and Ventilation</u>: Underground mines require adequate support systems to ensure the safety of workers and maintain stability in the mine workings. Ventilation systems are also essential to provide fresh air and remove harmful gases and dust generated during mining operations.

Underground mining in Emalahleni offers advantages such as higher ore grades, lower environmental impact on the surface, and greater safety for workers compared to open-pit mining. However, it also poses challenges such as higher operating costs, logistical complexities, and safety hazards associated with working underground.

In summary, both open-pit and underground mining techniques play vital roles in the extraction of coal and minerals in Emalahleni. While open-pit mining is well-suited for shallow deposits and offers high productivity, underground mining is necessary for accessing deeper reserves and minimising environmental impacts on the surface. By employing a combination of these techniques and adhering to best practices in mine planning, operation, and rehabilitation, the mining industry in Emalahleni can strive to achieve sustainable resource extraction while minimising its environmental footprint and maximising its socio-economic benefits for local communities.

Mining activities, including both open-pit and underground mining, can have significant environmental impacts that pose challenges to ecosystem health, biodiversity, and community well-being. These environmental considerations are crucial to address to ensure sustainable mining practices and minimize adverse effects on the environment. Some of the key environmental challenges associated with mining activities include:

Land Degradation: Mining operations often require the clearing of vegetation and soil removal, leading to land degradation and habitat loss. Open-pit mining, in particular, can result in large-scale disturbance of landscapes, altering natural ecosystems and reducing biodiversity. Reclamation and rehabilitation efforts are essential to restore mined areas and mitigate land degradation.

Air and Water Pollution Mining activities can release pollutants into the air and water, posing risks to human health and ecosystem integrity. Dust emissions from blasting, drilling, and hauling operations can contribute to air pollution, affecting air quality and respiratory health. Similarly, runoff from mining sites can contain sediment, heavy metals, and other contaminants, polluting surface water sources and aquatic habitats. Implementation of effective dust control measures and water management practices, such as sedimentation ponds and water treatment facilities, can help mitigate these impacts.

Water Consumption and Depletion: Mining operations require significant quantities of water for various purposes, including mineral processing, dust suppression, and worker hydration. Excessive water consumption can strain local water resources, leading to depletion of aquifers, reduced stream flow, and impacts on downstream ecosystems. Adopting water recycling and conservation measures, as well as implementing sustainable water management practices, can help minimize water consumption and mitigate the risk of water scarcity.

Soil Contamination: Mining activities can result in soil contamination through the release of chemicals and heavy metals from ore processing and waste disposal. Contaminated soils can pose risks to human health, agricultural productivity, and ecosystem functioning. Implementing proper containment and remediation measures, such as soil capping, phytoremediation, and soil stabilization, can help mitigate soil contamination and protect environmental quality.

Erosion and Sedimentation: Mining operations can contribute to erosion and sedimentation, particularly in areas with steep slopes or fragile soils. Soil erosion can lead to the loss of fertile topsoil, increased sedimentation in water bodies, and degradation of aquatic habitats. Implementing erosion control measures, such as revegetation, terracing, and erosion barriers, can help minimize soil erosion and sedimentation and protect downstream ecosystems.

Climate Change Impacts: Mining activities can also contribute to climate change through the release of greenhouse gases, such as carbon dioxide and methane, from fossil fuel combustion, transportation, and energy consumption. Additionally, deforestation and land use changes associated with mining can exacerbate carbon emissions and disrupt carbon sequestration processes. Adopting cleaner energy technologies, promoting energy efficiency, and minimizing deforestation can help reduce the carbon footprint of mining operations and mitigate climate change impacts.

Addressing these environmental considerations and challenges associated with mining activities is essential to ensure responsible resource extraction and sustainable development. By implementing effective environmental management practices, adopting innovative technologies, and engaging with stakeholders, the mining industry can minimize its environmental footprint and mitigate adverse impacts on ecosystems, water resources, and communities.

Chapter 5: Socioeconomic Impacts

In Emalahleni, the mining industry has had profound social and economic consequences on local communities, shaping the region's identity, livelihoods, and well-being. Examining these consequences reveals both positive contributions and challenges faced by residents:

1. Employment and Economic Development:

- Positive Impact: Mining activities in Emalahleni have provided employment opportunities for local residents, contributing to economic growth and poverty reduction. Direct employment in mining operations, as well as indirect employment in supporting industries, has supported livelihoods and improved living standards for many families.

- Negative Impact: However, the dependence on mining as the primary economic driver has led to economic vulnerabilities, particularly during periods of market downturns or mine closures. The transient nature of mining employment and the risk of job displacement due to automation or restructuring can lead to economic instability and social tensions within communities.

2. Infrastructure Development:

- Positive Impact: The mining industry has invested in infrastructure development in Emalahleni, including roads, housing, healthcare facilities, and schools. Improved infrastructure has enhanced connectivity, access to services, and overall quality of life for residents.

- Negative Impact: Rapid infrastructure development can strain local resources and infrastructure capacity, leading to challenges such as increased traffic congestion, pressure on public services, and disparities in infrastructure provision between mining and non-mining areas. Moreover, infrastructure development may not always address the specific needs of marginalised or disadvantaged communities within Emalahleni.

3. Social Investment and Development:

- Positive Impact: Mining companies in Emalahleni have undertaken social responsibility initiatives to support local communities, including investments in education, healthcare, skills development, and community infrastructure. These initiatives have contributed to social upliftment, empowerment, and capacity-building in the region.

- Negative Impact: However, the effectiveness and inclusivity of social investment programs may vary, leading to unequal distribution of benefits and limited participation from marginalised groups within communities. Dependence on external funding and initiatives may also hinder the development of local capacity and self-reliance, perpetuating a cycle of dependency on mining companies for social support.

4. Cultural and Social Dynamics:

- Positive Impact: Mining activities in Emalahleni have brought together diverse cultures and communities, fostering social cohesion, cross-cultural exchange, and community pride. Events and festivals related to mining serve as platforms for cultural expression, celebration, and community bonding.

- Negative Impact: Rapid demographic changes and influxes of migrant workers associated with mining operations can disrupt traditional social structures and cultural practices, leading to tensions and conflicts within communities. Social isolation and alienation may occur among indigenous or marginalized groups who feel marginalized or excluded from the benefits of mining.

5. Health and Well-being:

- Positive Impact: Improved access to healthcare services and infrastructure, as well as employment opportunities with healthcare benefits, have contributed to enhanced health outcomes and well-being for residents in mining communities.

- Negative Impact: However, mining activities can also pose risks to health and safety, including occupational hazards, exposure to air and water pollution, and mental health impacts due to social disruption and economic uncertainty. Addressing these health risks requires comprehensive health monitoring, preventive measures, and access to healthcare services for affected communities.

The social and economic consequences of mining on local communities in Emalahleni are multifaceted, characterised by a mix of positive contributions and challenges. By fostering dialogue, collaboration, and partnership among stakeholders, mining companies, government authorities, and local communities can work together to maximise the positive impacts of mining while mitigating its negative consequences, ensuring sustainable development and well-being for all residents of Emalahleni.

In Emalahleni, the mining industry has a significant impact on employment opportunities, infrastructure development, and income disparities within the local communities. Understanding these aspects provides insights into the socio-economic dynamics and challenges faced by residents:

1. Employment Opportunities:

- The mining industry in Emalahleni provides a substantial number of direct and indirect employment opportunities for local residents. Jobs range from skilled positions such as engineers, geologists, and technicians to unskilled labor in areas like mining operations, construction, and services.

- However, the availability of mining-related jobs may fluctuate depending on factors such as market demand, technological advancements, and global commodity prices. During economic downturns or mine closures, residents may face job losses and reduced employment opportunities, leading to economic insecurity and social tensions within communities.

- Additionally, the transient nature of mining employment, characterized by temporary contracts and seasonal work, can contribute to job instability and uncertainty for workers, affecting their livelihoods and well-being.

2. Infrastructure Development:

- The mining industry plays a crucial role in infrastructure development in Emalahleni, with mining companies investing in roads, housing, healthcare facilities, schools, and other essential infrastructure projects.

- Improved infrastructure enhances connectivity, access to services, and overall quality of life for residents, contributing to social well-being and economic development. However, infrastructure development may not always address the specific needs of marginalized or disadvantaged communities within Emalahleni, leading to disparities in access to services and amenities.

- Moreover, rapid infrastructure development can strain local resources and infrastructure capacity, leading to challenges such as increased traffic congestion, pressure on public services, and environmental degradation.

3. Income Disparities:

- The mining industry in Emalahleni contributes to income disparities within local communities, with workers in the mining sector often earning higher salaries compared to those in other industries or sectors.

- While mining-related employment opportunities provide income for many residents, income disparities may arise between those employed in the formal mining sector and those engaged in informal or precarious work, such as small-scale mining, informal trading, or subsistence agriculture.

- Income disparities can also be influenced by factors such as education levels, skills, experience, and access to opportunities for career advancement. Marginalised or disadvantaged groups within communities, including women, youth, and people with disabilities, may face barriers to accessing well-paid employment in the mining sector, exacerbating income inequalities.

In conclusion, the mining industry in Emalahleni presents both opportunities and challenges in terms of employment, infrastructure development, and income distribution. While mining-related employment provides livelihoods for many residents and contributes to economic development, it also poses challenges such as job instability, infrastructure strain, and income disparities within communities. Addressing these challenges requires a comprehensive approach that fosters inclusive growth, equitable development, and sustainable livelihoods for all residents of Emalahleni.

Chapter 6: Environmental Concerns

Air Pollution:

Air pollution is a pervasive issue in Emalahleni, stemming from dust and particulate matter generated by mining operations. The process of extracting, transporting, and processing coal releases fine particles into the air, contributing to elevated levels of air pollution in the region. Additionally, the combustion of fossil fuels for energy generation and transportation emits pollutants such as sulfur dioxide (SO_2) and nitrogen oxides (NO_x), further exacerbating air quality issues. High levels of air pollution pose significant risks to human health, particularly respiratory and cardiovascular diseases, and can have detrimental effects on vulnerable populations, including children, the elderly, and individuals with pre-existing health conditions. Moreover, air pollution can impact the environment by causing acid rain, damaging vegetation, and contributing to the formation of smog and haze, which reduce visibility and degrade ecosystems.

Water Pollution:

Water pollution is another major environmental concern associated with mining activities in Emalahleni. The release of contaminants from mining operations, including heavy metals, acids, and toxic chemicals, can contaminate surface and groundwater sources, posing risks to both human health and aquatic ecosystems. Acid mine drainage (AMD), a byproduct of sulfide mineral oxidation, is a significant contributor to water pollution in mining-affected areas. AMD is characterized by low pH levels and high concentrations of heavy metals, which can have devastating effects on aquatic life and water quality. Moreover, sedimentation from mining activities can increase turbidity in water bodies, smothering aquatic habitats and impairing ecosystem function. The contamination of water sources not only jeopardizes aquatic biodiversity but also undermines access to clean water for drinking, agriculture, and sanitation, posing serious risks to human health and socio-economic development in the region.

Land Degradation:

Land degradation is a pervasive environmental issue in Emalahleni, driven by the extensive land disturbance and habitat loss associated with mining operations. Open-pit mining activities involve the removal of vegetation, soil, and rock to access coal seams, resulting in large-scale alterations to the landscape. The conversion of natural habitats into mining sites not only diminishes the aesthetic value of the land but also disrupts ecological processes and reduces biodiversity. Moreover, soil erosion, compaction, and subsidence associated with mining activities further degrade land quality, leading to reduced soil fertility, loss of agricultural productivity, and degradation of land for future land uses. Land degradation has far-reaching consequences for ecosystem health, food security, and socio-economic well-being in Emalahleni, exacerbating environmental vulnerabilities and undermining the resilience of local communities.

Habitat Destruction:

Habitat destruction is a significant environmental consequence of mining activities in Emalahleni, as mining operations encroach upon critical ecosystems and wildlife habitats. The construction of infrastructure, such as roads, railways, and pipelines, to support mining activities fragments habitats, restricts wildlife movement, and diminishes connectivity between natural areas. The loss of habitat and biodiversity undermines ecosystem services, such as pollination, soil fertility, and water purification, compromising the resilience of local ecosystems and exacerbating environmental degradation. Moreover, habitat destruction can have cascading effects on species populations, leading to declines in biodiversity and ecosystem function. The loss of habitat and biodiversity threatens the long-term sustainability of ecosystems and undermines efforts to conserve and protect natural resources in Emalahleni.

The environmental impacts of mining in Emalahleni, including air and water pollution, land degradation, and habitat destruction, are significant and multifaceted. Addressing these impacts requires a comprehensive approach that integrates pollution prevention, mitigation measures, and ecosystem restoration efforts to minimize harm to the environment and promote sustainable development. By adopting responsible mining practices, embracing innovation, and engaging stakeholders, Emalahleni can strive to mitigate its environmental footprint and safeguard the natural heritage for future generations.

Environmental Monitoring and Regulation:

- One of the primary efforts to mitigate environmental effects in Emalahleni is through robust environmental monitoring and regulation. Government agencies, such as the Department of Mineral Resources and Energy and the Department of Environment, Forestry, and Fisheries, enforce regulations and standards to minimize pollution and protect natural resources.

- Environmental Impact Assessments (EIAs) are conducted for mining projects to assess potential environmental impacts and develop mitigation measures. These assessments evaluate factors such as air and water quality, soil stability, and biodiversity, ensuring that mining activities comply with environmental laws and regulations.

Pollution Prevention and Control Measures:

- Mining companies in Emalahleni implement pollution prevention and control measures to minimize the release of contaminants into the environment. Technologies such as dust suppression systems, water treatment facilities, and waste management practices are employed to reduce pollution from mining operations.

- Advanced equipment and machinery with lower emissions are used to minimize air pollution from mining activities. Additionally, measures such as covering stockpiles, revegetating disturbed areas, and implementing erosion control measures help prevent land degradation and habitat destruction.

Rehabilitation and Restoration Efforts:

- Rehabilitation and restoration of mined areas are essential components of environmental mitigation efforts in Emalahleni. Mining companies are required to develop and implement rehabilitation plans to restore mined land to a sustainable condition after mining operations cease.

- Techniques such as land reclamation, revegetation, and soil stabilization are employed to rehabilitate mined sites and restore ecological function. Rehabilitation efforts aim to promote biodiversity, restore ecosystem services, and mitigate the long-term impacts of mining on the environment.

Community Engagement and Participation:

- Engaging local communities in environmental management and decision-making processes is crucial for effective mitigation efforts in Emalahleni. Community members are often directly impacted by mining activities and have valuable insights and knowledge about local environmental issues.

- Mining companies collaborate with local stakeholders, including community leaders, non-governmental organizations (NGOs), and government agencies, to develop sustainable mining practices and address environmental concerns. Community participation fosters transparency, accountability, and social responsibility in environmental management initiatives.

Research and Innovation:

- Research and innovation play a vital role in developing new technologies and approaches to mitigate environmental effects in Emalahleni. Collaborative research projects between mining companies, academic institutions, and research organizations aim to identify innovative solutions to environmental challenges.

- Technologies such as renewable energy systems, carbon capture and storage (CCS), and sustainable water management practices are explored to reduce the environmental footprint of mining operations. Research findings inform policy development, industry best practices, and technological advancements in environmental mitigation.

Efforts to mitigate environmental effects of mining in the Emalahleni local community are multifaceted and ongoing. Environmental monitoring and regulation, pollution prevention and control measures, rehabilitation and restoration efforts, community engagement, and research and innovation are key components of environmental mitigation strategies. By implementing these initiatives collaboratively and comprehensively, Emalahleni can strive to achieve sustainable mining practices that balance economic development with environmental conservation. Moving forward, continued commitment to environmental stewardship and sustainable development is essential to safeguarding the natural heritage and well-being of future generations in Emalahleni.

Chapter 7: Regulation and Governance

The Department of Mineral Resources (DMR) in South Africa plays a crucial role in regulating and overseeing the mining sector, including in Emalahleni. The DMR's framework encompasses various components aimed at promoting responsible mining practices, ensuring compliance with legislation, and fostering sustainable development. Below is an overview of the key elements of the DMR's framework:

Legislation and Policy Development:

- The DMR is responsible for developing and implementing legislation and policies related to mineral resources and mining activities in South Africa. This includes the Mineral and Petroleum Resources Development Act (MPRDA) and its associated regulations, which govern the exploration, extraction, benefaction, and utilization of mineral resources.

- The DMR also develops policies and guidelines to guide the implementation of mining regulations, address emerging issues, and promote sustainable development in the mining sector.

Mining Rights Administration:

- The DMR is responsible for administering mining rights, licenses, and permits in South Africa, including in Emalahleni. This includes processing applications for prospecting rights, mining rights, and mining permits, as well as monitoring compliance with the terms and conditions of these rights.

- The DMR oversees the allocation of mineral rights, conducts reviews of mining rights applications, and facilitates the transfer of rights between parties, ensuring transparency, equity, and accountability in the allocation of mineral resources.

Environmental Regulation and Compliance:

- The DMR works in collaboration with the Department of Environment, Forestry, and Fisheries (DEFF) to regulate and enforce environmental standards in the mining sector. This includes conducting environmental impact assessments (EIAs) for mining projects, issuing environmental authorizations, and monitoring compliance with environmental regulations.

- The DMR ensures that mining activities adhere to environmental management plans, rehabilitation requirements, and pollution prevention measures, mitigating the environmental impacts of mining and promoting environmental sustainability.

Health and Safety Oversight:

- The DMR oversees health and safety standards in the mining sector to protect the health and well-being of mine workers and prevent accidents and occupational hazards. This includes enforcing compliance with the Mine Health and Safety Act (MHSA) and conducting inspections and audits of mining operations.

- The DMR works closely with industry stakeholders, labor organizations, and regulatory bodies to promote a culture of safety, implement best practices, and address health and safety challenges in the mining sector.

Community Engagement and Social Responsibility:

- The DMR promotes community engagement and social responsibility in the mining sector, emphasising the importance of consultation, collaboration, and partnerships with local communities and stakeholders.

- The DMR requires mining companies to develop Social and Labour Plans (SLPs) as part of their mining rights applications, outlining their commitments to socio-economic development, employment creation, and community empowerment in mining-affected areas.

Monitoring and Enforcement:

- The DMR conducts monitoring, inspections, and enforcement activities to ensure compliance with mining regulations and standards. This includes conducting regular site visits, audits, and investigations to assess mining operations' adherence to legal requirements and address non-compliance issues.

- The DMR has enforcement powers to impose sanctions, fines, and penalties on mining companies found to be in violation of mining regulations, promoting accountability and deterrence of non-compliance.

Department of Mineral Resources (DMR) framework in South Africa provides the regulatory framework and oversight mechanisms necessary to promote responsible mining practices, protect the environment, and foster sustainable development in Emalahleni and across the country. Through collaboration with industry stakeholders, government agencies, and local communities, the DMR aims to ensure that mining activities contribute positively to economic growth, social development, and environmental stewardship while minimizing negative impacts on communities and ecosystems.

The oversight of mining operations involves multiple stakeholders, including government agencies, industry stakeholders, and community organizations, each playing a distinct role in ensuring responsible and sustainable mining practices. An analysis of their roles reveals the complex interplay between regulatory compliance, environmental protection, socio-economic development, and community engagement:

Government Agencies:

- Government agencies, such as the Department of Mineral Resources (DMR) and the Department of Environment, Forestry, and Fisheries (DEFF), have a primary role in regulating and overseeing mining operations. These agencies develop and enforce legislation, policies, and regulations governing the mining sector.

- The DMR administers mining rights, licenses, and permits, conducts inspections and audits, and ensures compliance with health, safety, and environmental standards. The DEFF is responsible for conducting environmental impact assessments (EIAs), issuing environmental authorizations, and monitoring environmental compliance.

- Government agencies also play a crucial role in facilitating stakeholder engagement, resolving disputes, and promoting transparency and accountability in the mining sector.

Industry Stakeholders:

- Industry stakeholders, including mining companies, industry associations, and trade unions, are responsible for implementing mining operations in compliance with regulatory requirements and industry best practices.

- Mining companies develop and implement environmental management plans, health and safety protocols, and community engagement strategies to mitigate the environmental and social impacts of mining operations. Industry associations, such as the Chamber of Mines, provide guidance, support, and advocacy for mining companies, promoting industry standards and best practices.

- Trade unions represent the interests of mine workers, advocating for fair wages, safe working conditions, and labor rights. They engage with mining companies and government agencies to address labor issues, promote workforce development, and ensure worker participation in decision-making processes.

Community Organizations:

- Community organizations, including non-governmental organizations (NGOs), community-based organizations (CBOs), and traditional authorities, play a vital role in representing the interests and concerns of local communities affected by mining operations.

- These organizations advocate for community rights, environmental justice, and social equity, seeking to ensure that mining activities benefit local residents and respect their cultural, social, and economic rights. They engage with mining companies, government agencies, and other stakeholders to negotiate agreements, raise awareness, and address community needs and grievances.

- Traditional authorities, such as chiefs and traditional councils, often play a central role in community governance and decision-making, representing the interests of indigenous and traditional communities and promoting sustainable development initiatives.

The oversight of mining operations requires collaboration and cooperation among government agencies, industry stakeholders, and community organizations to ensure responsible and sustainable mining practices. Government agencies provide regulatory oversight and enforcement, industry stakeholders implement operational standards and best practices, and community organizations advocate for community rights and environmental protection. By working together, these stakeholders can address the complex challenges associated with mining operations, promote socio-economic development, and safeguard the environment and well-being of affected communities.

Chapter 8: Challenges, Corruption and Future Prospects

The mining industry in Emalahleni faces several significant challenges that impact its operations, sustainability, and relationships with stakeholders. These challenges include:

Depletion of Resources:

- Emalahleni has long been known for its abundant coal reserves, which have been the primary focus of mining activities in the region. However, the depletion of easily accessible coal reserves poses a significant challenge for the mining industry.

- As mining companies exhaust high-quality coal seams, they must contend with declining ore grades, increased operational costs, and the need to invest in more advanced extraction technologies. This can lead to reduced profitability and competitiveness in the global market.

Regulatory Compliance:

- The regulatory environment governing mining activities in Emalahleni is complex and evolving, requiring mining companies to navigate a range of legislative requirements, environmental standards, and community engagement obligations.

- Ensuring compliance with regulations related to environmental management, health and safety, social responsibility, and community development poses challenges for mining companies. Failure to meet regulatory requirements can result in fines, penalties, and repetitional damage.

Community Opposition

- Community opposition to mining activities has emerged as a significant challenge in Emalahleni, as local residents and environmental activists raise concerns about the environmental and social impacts of mining.

- Communities affected by mining operations may oppose new mining projects or expansion plans due to concerns about air and water pollution, land degradation, loss of agricultural land, displacement of communities, and cultural heritage impacts.

- Community opposition can lead to delays in obtaining permits and approvals, increased regulatory scrutiny, legal disputes, and repetitional risks for mining companies.

Economic Diversification:

- Emalahleni's economy has historically been heavily reliant on the mining industry, making it vulnerable to fluctuations in commodity prices, market demand, and regulatory changes.

- Diversifying the local economy away from dependence on mining presents a challenge for Emalahleni, as alternative industries and economic opportunities may be limited. Transitioning to sustainable industries such as renewable energy, tourism, and manufacturing requires investment, infrastructure development, and skills training.

Environmental Sustainability:

- Ensuring environmental sustainability is a growing concern for the mining industry in Emalahleni, as stakeholders increasingly demand responsible mining practices and environmental stewardship.

- Mining operations in Emalahleni must address environmental challenges such as air and water pollution, land degradation, habitat destruction, and greenhouse gas emissions. Implementing effective environmental management strategies and rehabilitation efforts is essential to mitigate these impacts and restore ecosystems.

Social License to Operate:

- Maintaining a social license to operate is critical for the long-term success and sustainability of mining operations in Emalahleni. Building trust and positive relationships with local communities, stakeholders, and government authorities is essential to secure support for mining projects.

- Engaging in meaningful dialogue, addressing community concerns, and implementing community development initiatives are key strategies for earning and maintaining social acceptance and support for mining activities.

The mining industry in Emalahleni faces numerous challenges, including resource depletion, regulatory compliance, community opposition, economic diversification, environmental sustainability, and social license to operate. Addressing these challenges requires collaboration, innovation, and responsible leadership from mining companies, government agencies, and local communities to ensure the long-term viability and sustainability of mining operations in the region.

Corruption within the human resources (HR) function of mining companies can have detrimental effects on organizational culture, employee morale, and overall performance. Here are some ways corruption may manifest within the HR department of a mining company:

Bribery and Nepotism in Hiring Practices:

- Corruption in HR may involve accepting bribes or kickbacks from job applicants or recruitment agencies in exchange for employment opportunities. This unethical practice undermines fair and merit-based recruitment processes, favouring individuals with connections or financial resources over qualified candidates.

- Nepotism, where hiring decisions are based on familial or personal relationships rather than qualifications and experience, can also contribute to corruption within HR departments. This erodes trust among employees and creates a perception of favouritism and unfair treatment.

Payroll Fraud and Embezzlement:

- HR departments are responsible for managing payroll and employee benefits, making them vulnerable to corruption schemes such as payroll fraud and embezzlement. This may involve inflating employee salaries, creating fictitious employees, or diverting funds meant for employee benefits into personal accounts.

- Embezzlement of company funds by HR personnel can have significant financial consequences for the mining company, leading to financial losses, reduced employee morale, and damage to the company's reputation.

Discrimination and Harassment:

- Corruption in HR may also manifest in discriminatory practices and workplace harassment. HR personnel may engage in discriminatory hiring or promotion practices based on factors such as race, gender, or ethnicity, violating anti-discrimination laws and perpetuating inequality in the workplace.

- Additionally, HR personnel may fail to address complaints of harassment or misconduct appropriately, covering up incidents to protect the company's reputation or the perpetrators involved. This can create a toxic work environment and undermine employee trust in the HR department's ability to uphold employee rights and well-being.

Conflict of Interest and Favouritism:

- HR personnel may engage in conflicts of interest or favouritism by showing preferential treatment to certain employees or stakeholders in exchange for personal gain or benefits. This can include providing job opportunities, promotions, or favourable treatment to individuals with whom HR personnel have personal or financial relationships.

- Such actions erode trust in HR's impartiality and integrity, undermining employee morale and contributing to a culture of cynicism and disengagement within the organisation.

Addressing corruption within the HR function of mining companies requires robust measures to promote transparency, accountability, and ethical conduct. This includes implementing clear policies and procedures for recruitment, hiring, and employee management, providing ethics training for HR personnel, establishing channels for reporting misconduct, and conducting regular audits to detect and prevent fraudulent activities. By fostering a culture of integrity and accountability within the HR department, mining companies can uphold ethical standards and promote a fair and inclusive workplace environment for all employees.

When community leaders prioritize personal interests and numerous unregistered community forums exist, it can exacerbate existing challenges and hinder effective governance and development in mining-affected areas like Emalahleni. Here's how these factors can impact the community:

Divided Community Representation:

- The presence of multiple unregistered community forums, often led by individuals serving personal interests, can fragment community representation and leadership. This fragmentation undermines efforts to establish unified community voices and negotiate effectively with mining companies, government agencies, and other stakeholders.

- Conflicting agendas and lack of coordination among these forums can lead to discord, competition for resources, and difficulty in reaching consensus on critical issues affecting the community.

Lack of Accountability and Transparency:

- Unregistered community forums may operate without formal oversight or accountability mechanisms, making it challenging to ensure transparency and integrity in decision-making processes. Leaders of these forums may prioritize their own interests over those of the broader community, leading to a lack of trust and legitimacy.

- Without formal registration or recognition, there may be limited avenues for community members to hold leaders accountable for their actions or challenge decisions that are not in the community's best interests.

Marginalisation of Certain Groups:

- In communities with unregistered forums, certain groups or individuals may be excluded or marginalised from participating in decision-making processes. This can perpetuate inequalities based on factors such as gender, ethnicity, or socioeconomic status, further marginalising vulnerable populations within the community.

- The voices of marginalised groups may be overlooked or disregarded, leading to disparities in access to resources, representation, and opportunities for participation in community development initiatives.

Ineffective Engagement with Stakeholders:

- Unregistered community forums may struggle to engage effectively with external stakeholders, including mining companies, government agencies, and civil society organizations. This can limit the community's ability to advocate for its interests, negotiate benefits agreements, or address grievances related to mining activities.

- Without formal recognition or representation, these forums may lack the legitimacy and credibility needed to effectively engage with stakeholders and influence decision-making processes at the local or regional level.

Risk of Exploitation and Manipulation:

- Community leaders serving personal interests within unregistered forums may be susceptible to exploitation or manipulation by external actors, such as mining companies or political interests. This can undermine the autonomy and independence of community leadership structures, compromising their ability to represent the community's interests effectively.

- External actors may seek to co-opt or influence community leaders for their own gain, further undermining the community's ability to assert its rights and negotiate fair terms for resource extraction and development projects.

Addressing these challenges requires concerted efforts to strengthen community governance structures, promote transparency and accountability, and foster inclusive and participatory decision-making processes. This may involve supporting the formal registration and recognition of community forums, providing training and capacity-building for community leaders, and facilitating dialogue and collaboration among diverse community stakeholders. By promoting democratic governance and empowering communities to advocate for their interests collectively, mining-affected areas like Emalahleni can work towards achieving more equitable and sustainable development outcomes.

The future of the mining sector, including in regions like Emalahleni, depends on embracing diversification and adopting sustainable practices to address environmental, social, and economic challenges. Here's a discussion of potential future directions for the mining sector:

Diversification of Mineral Resources:

- As traditional resources like coal become depleted or face declining demand due to environmental concerns, there is a need to diversify the mineral resources extracted in Emalahleni. This could involve exploring and developing new mineral deposits such as rare earth elements, lithium, and platinum group metals, which are increasingly in demand for renewable energy technologies, electric vehicles, and other emerging industries.

- Diversification can reduce reliance on a single commodity and make the mining sector more resilient to market fluctuations and shifts in global demand. It also opens up opportunities for innovation, investment, and economic growth in new sectors.

Transition to Sustainable Energy and Minerals:

- The transition to a low-carbon economy presents opportunities for the mining sector to contribute to renewable energy production and energy storage technologies. This includes extracting minerals such as lithium, cobalt, and graphite used in batteries for electric vehicles and renewable energy storage systems.

- Embracing sustainable energy and minerals can position Emalahleni as a hub for clean energy production and mineral processing, driving economic diversification and job creation while reducing reliance on fossil fuels and mitigating environmental impacts.

Adoption of Green Mining Technologies:

- Green mining technologies, such as renewable energy sources, water recycling systems, and advanced automation and digitisation, can minimize the environmental footprint of mining operations. Embracing these technologies can reduce energy consumption, water usage, and greenhouse gas emissions, while improving operational efficiency and productivity.

- Investing in research and development of green mining technologies can position Emalahleni as a leader in sustainable mining practices, attracting investment and expertise from around the world.

Community Engagement and Benefit Sharing:

- Future directions for the mining sector should prioritise meaningful engagement with local communities and stakeholders, ensuring that mining activities contribute to sustainable development and benefit local residents. This includes implementing robust social and labor programs, investing in education, healthcare, and infrastructure, and promoting economic opportunities for local businesses and entrepreneurs.

- Building strong partnerships between mining companies, government agencies, and community organisations can foster trust, collaboration, and shared decision-making, leading to more inclusive and equitable outcomes for all stakeholders.

Environmental Rehabilitation and Ecosystem Restoration:

- Mining companies should prioritise environmental rehabilitation and ecosystem restoration efforts to mitigate the impacts of past mining activities and restore degraded landscapes. This includes reclamation of mined land, revegetation, water management, and biodiversity conservation measures.

- Investing in long-term environmental stewardship can enhance the resilience of ecosystems, protect water resources, and preserve biodiversity, ensuring that mining activities are conducted in harmony with nature and leave a positive legacy for future generations.

The future of the mining sector in Emalahleni lies in embracing diversification, adopting sustainable practices, and fostering inclusive and responsible development. By leveraging emerging opportunities in clean energy, green technologies, and community engagement, Emalahleni can position itself as a model for sustainable mining and contribute to a more resilient and equitable future for mining-affected regions around the world.

Chapter 9: Case Studies

Here is an in-depth examination of specific mining projects or companies operating in Emalahleni, highlighting their impact on the local community and environment:

1. **Exxaro Resources Limited**:
- Exxaro operates several coal mines in the Emalahleni area, including the Grootegeluk, Leeuwpan, and Matla mines.
- Impact on the Local Community: Exxaro has implemented community development initiatives, including skills development programs, infrastructure projects, and social investment initiatives. The company has created employment opportunities and supported local businesses, contributing to socio-economic development in the region.
- Environmental Impact: Exxaro has faced criticism for environmental issues, including air and water pollution, land degradation, and biodiversity loss associated with its mining activities. The company has implemented environmental management plans and rehabilitation efforts to mitigate these impacts, but challenges remain in ensuring effective environmental stewardship.

2. **Seriti Resources**:
- Seriti Resources acquired several coal assets from Anglo American, including the New Vaal, New Denmark, and Kriel mines.
- Impact on the Local Community: Seriti emphasizes its commitment to sustainable development and responsible mining practices, including community engagement and development initiatives. The company has implemented social investment programs, job creation initiatives, and enterprise development projects to support local communities and promote inclusive growth.
- Environmental Impact: Seriti faces environmental challenges associated with coal mining, including air and water pollution, land degradation, and habitat destruction. The company has implemented environmental management systems and rehabilitation efforts to

minimize its environmental footprint and comply with regulatory requirements.

3. **South32**:

- South32 operates the Khutala, Klipspruit, and Wolvekrans collieries in the Emalahleni area.

- Impact on the Local Community: South32 has engaged with local communities through stakeholder consultations, social investment programs, and community development initiatives. The company has supported education, healthcare, and infrastructure projects, contributing to socio-economic development and empowerment in surrounding communities.

- Environmental Impact: South32 faces environmental challenges related to coal mining, including air and water pollution, land degradation, and ecosystem disturbance. The company has implemented environmental management plans and rehabilitation efforts to minimize its environmental impact and ensure compliance with environmental regulations.

4. **Glencore**:

- Glencore operates the Goedgevonden and Impunzi coal mines in the Emalahleni area.

- Impact on the Local Community: Glencore has implemented community development initiatives, including skills training programs, small business support, and social investment projects. The company has created employment opportunities and supported local economic development, contributing to the well-being of surrounding communities.

- Environmental Impact: Glencore faces environmental challenges associated with coal mining operations, including air and water pollution, land degradation, and biodiversity impacts. The company has implemented environmental management systems and rehabilitation efforts to mitigate these impacts and promote sustainable environmental practices.

5. **Anglo American**:

- Anglo American previously operated several coal mines in the Emalahleni area before divesting these assets to Seriti Resources.

- Impact on the Local Community: Anglo American implemented community development initiatives during its tenure in Emalahleni, including social investment programs, skills development initiatives, and infrastructure projects. The company contributed to local economic development and supported community empowerment efforts.

- Environmental Impact: Anglo American faced environmental challenges associated with coal mining, including air and water pollution, land degradation, and habitat destruction. The company implemented environmental management plans and rehabilitation efforts to address these challenges and minimize its environmental footprint.

6. **Sasol Mining**:

- Sasol Mining operates coal mines and coal-to-liquid (CTL) facilities in the Emalahleni area.

- Impact on the Local Community: Sasol Mining has implemented community development initiatives, including skills training programs, education support, and small business development projects. The company has created employment opportunities and supported local economic growth, contributing to the socio-economic well-being of surrounding communities.

- Environmental Impact: Sasol Mining faces environmental challenges associated with coal mining and CTL operations, including air and water pollution, land degradation, and greenhouse gas emissions. The company has implemented environmental management systems and mitigation measures to address these impacts and comply with environmental regulations.

7. **Universal Coal**:

- Universal Coal operates the Kangala and New Clydesdale collieries in the Emalahleni area.

- Impact on the Local Community: Universal Coal has engaged with local communities through social investment programs, job creation initiatives, and infrastructure development projects. The company has contributed to socio-economic development and empowerment in surrounding communities, creating opportunities for local residents.

- Environmental Impact: Universal Coal faces environmental challenges associated with coal mining, including air and water pollution, land degradation, and biodiversity impacts. The company has implemented environmental management plans and rehabilitation efforts to minimize its environmental footprint and ensure compliance with regulatory requirements.

8. **Wescoal Holdings Limited**:

- Wescoal Holdings operates several coal mines in the Emalahleni area, including the Elandspruit and Khanyisa collieries.

- Impact on the Local Community: Wescoal Holdings has implemented community development initiatives, including skills development programs, infrastructure projects, and social investment initiatives. The company has created employment opportunities and supported local economic development, contributing to the well-being of surrounding communities.

- Environmental Impact: Wescoal Holdings faces environmental challenges associated with coal mining operations, including air and water pollution, land degradation, and habitat disturbance. The company has implemented environmental management systems and rehabilitation efforts to address these challenges and minimize its environmental impact.

9. **Canyon Coal**:

- Canyon Coal operates the Khanye and Phalanndwa collieries in the Emalahleni area.

- Impact on the Local Community: Canyon Coal has engaged with local communities through social investment programs, job creation initiatives, and enterprise development projects. The company has contributed to socio-economic development and empowerment in surrounding communities, creating opportunities for local residents.

- Environmental Impact: Canyon Coal faces environmental challenges associated with coal mining, including air and water pollution, land degradation, and ecosystem disturbance. The company has implemented environmental management plans and rehabilitation efforts to minimize its environmental footprint and ensure compliance with regulatory requirements.

10. **Kangra Coal**:

- Kangra Coal operates the Savmore and Welgedacht collieries in the Emalahleni area.

- Impact on the Local Community: Kangra Coal has implemented community development initiatives, including skills training programs, education support, and social investment projects. The company has created employment opportunities and supported local economic development.

In 2019, Seriti Resources announced its acquisition of South32's South African Energy Coal (SAEC) business, which includes coal assets in the Witbank coalfield in Emalahleni. This acquisition marked a significant development in the South African mining industry and had implications for the local community, the environment, and the broader coal market. Here is an examination of Seriti's acquisition of South32's coal assets and its potential impact:

Business Consolidation:

- The acquisition of South32's SAEC business by Seriti Resources represented a consolidation of coal assets in the Emalahleni region. This consolidation aimed to create a more competitive and sustainable coal mining operation under Seriti's ownership.

- By combining South32's coal assets with its existing portfolio, Seriti became one of the largest coal producers in South Africa, with a diverse portfolio of mines supplying both domestic and export markets.

Impact on the Local Community:

- The acquisition had implications for the local community in Emalahleni, as it affected employment, community development initiatives, and relationships with stakeholders.

- Seriti Resources pledged to continue South32's community engagement and development programs, including job creation initiatives, skills development projects, and social investment programs. However, there may have been concerns among local residents about potential changes in employment opportunities and the company's commitment to community development under new ownership.

Environmental Considerations:

- The acquisition raised environmental considerations related to the impact of coal mining on air and water quality, land degradation, and biodiversity in the Emalahleni region.

- Seriti Resources inherited South32's environmental management obligations and responsibilities, including compliance with regulatory requirements, implementation of environmental monitoring programs, and rehabilitation of mined areas. Ensuring effective environmental stewardship and mitigating the environmental impacts of coal mining operations remained critical priorities for Seriti.

Market Dynamics:

- The acquisition of South32's coal assets by Seriti Resources had implications for the broader coal market in South Africa and globally.

- Seriti's expanded coal portfolio positioned the company as a major player in the South African coal industry, with increased market share and influence. This consolidation may have implications for competition, pricing dynamics, and market trends in the coal sector.

Long-Term Sustainability:

- The success of Seriti's acquisition of South32's coal assets depended on its ability to manage the transition effectively, optimize operations, and navigate market challenges.

- Ensuring the long-term sustainability of coal mining operations in Emalahleni required a commitment to responsible mining practices, community engagement, environmental stewardship, and compliance with regulatory requirements.

Overall, Seriti's acquisition of South32's coal assets in Emalahleni represented a significant development in the South African mining industry. The impact of this acquisition on the local community, the environment, and the broader coal market depended on Seriti's ability to manage the transition effectively and uphold its commitments to sustainable mining practices and stakeholder engagement. Ongoing monitoring and evaluation of Seriti's operations would be necessary to assess its performance and adherence to environmental and social standards.

Chapter 10: Conclusion

In summary, the examination of specific mining projects and companies operating in Emalahleni, South Africa, reveals several key findings and insights:

Emalahleni hosts a diverse range of mining companies, including major players like Exxaro Resources Limited, Seriti Resources, and Glencore, as well as smaller operators like Canyon Coal and Wescoal Holdings Limited.

Mining companies in Emalahleni engage with local communities through various initiatives, including skills development programs, infrastructure projects, and social investment initiatives. However, challenges remain in addressing community needs and ensuring inclusive growth.

Coal mining activities in Emalahleni have significant environmental implications, including air and water pollution, land degradation, and biodiversity loss. Companies implement environmental management plans and rehabilitation efforts, but further improvements are necessary to mitigate environmental impacts effectively.

Regulatory compliance is a critical aspect of mining operations in Emalahleni, with companies facing challenges in navigating complex regulatory frameworks and ensuring adherence to environmental and safety standards.

The coal market in Emalahleni is influenced by global demand trends, coal prices, and regulatory changes. Companies must adapt to market dynamics and seek opportunities for sustainable growth and competitiveness.

Mining activities contribute to socio-economic development in Emalahleni by creating employment opportunities, supporting local businesses, and investing in community development initiatives. However, efforts to address socio-economic challenges and promote inclusive growth require continued commitment and collaboration.

The future of the mining sector in Emalahleni depends on embracing diversification, adopting sustainable practices, and fostering inclusive development. Companies must prioritise environmental stewardship, community engagement, and regulatory compliance to ensure long-term sustainability and positive outcomes for all stakeholders.

Reflecting on the future of mining in Emalahleni and its implications for the community and beyond, several key reflections emerge:

- Emalahleni's economy has long been dependent on the mining industry, particularly coal mining. As coal reserves deplete and global demand shifts towards cleaner energy sources, there is a need to diversify the local economy to reduce dependence on mining.

- Diversification efforts could focus on developing alternative industries such as renewable energy, tourism, agriculture, and manufacturing. This would create new economic opportunities, reduce vulnerability to fluctuations in the mining sector, and promote long-term sustainability.

- The future of mining in Emalahleni must prioritize the well-being and empowerment of local communities. Mining activities have both positive and negative impacts on communities, including employment opportunities, infrastructure development, and environmental degradation.

- It is crucial to invest in community development initiatives, including education, healthcare, housing, and skills training, to improve living standards and promote socio-economic inclusion. Empowering local communities to participate in decision-making processes and benefit from mining activities is essential for sustainable development.

- Mining activities in Emalahleni have significant environmental impacts, including air and water pollution, land degradation, and habitat destruction. The future of mining must prioritize environmental sustainability and adopt responsible mining practices to minimize these impacts.

- This involves implementing measures to reduce emissions, improve water management, rehabilitate mined areas, and preserve biodiversity. Investing in clean technologies and renewable energy solutions can help mitigate the environmental footprint of mining operations.

- Addressing the complex challenges associated with mining in Emalahleni requires collaboration and engagement with various stakeholders, including government, industry, civil society, and local communities.

- Open dialogue, transparency, and shared decision-making processes are essential to build trust, address concerns, and find mutually beneficial solutions. Engaging stakeholders in the planning, implementation, and monitoring of mining projects fosters social acceptance and promotes sustainable development.

- The future of mining in Emalahleni is influenced by global trends, including shifts towards renewable energy, decarbonisation efforts, and evolving regulatory frameworks.

- Companies operating in Emalahleni must adapt to these trends by embracing innovation, improving efficiency, and reducing environmental impact. Policymakers play a crucial role in shaping the regulatory environment and supporting the transition to a more sustainable and inclusive mining sector.

In conclusion, the future of mining in Emalahleni holds both challenges and opportunities for the community and beyond. By prioritising economic diversification, community well-being, environmental sustainability, stakeholder collaboration, and adaptation to global trends, Emalahleni can build a resilient and prosperous future that benefits all stakeholders involved.

Appendix A: Glossary of Key Terms

1. **Opencast Mining**: A surface mining technique where minerals are extracted from the surface of the earth through an open pit or borrow.

2. **Underground Mining**: Mining method used to extract minerals or ores that are located deep underground. It involves accessing the orebody through shafts, tunnels, or drifts.

3. **Coal Seam**: A layer of coal within a coal deposit, typically formed by the accumulation of plant material over millions of years.

4. **Geological Formation**: A distinct layer or unit of rock with characteristic lithology, structure, and age.

5. **Coal Reserves**: Estimated quantities of coal that can be economically mined from a deposit using current technology and under prevailing economic conditions.

6. **Environmental Impact Assessment** (EIA): A process of evaluating the potential environmental consequences of a proposed project or development, including mining activities, to inform decision-making and mitigate adverse impacts.

7. **Rehabilitation**: The process of restoring land and ecosystems affected by mining activities to a state suitable for future land use, including reclamation of disturbed land, soil stabilization, and revegetation.

8. **Social Impact Assessment** (SIA): An evaluation of the potential social impacts of a proposed project or development on local communities, including aspects such as employment, health, education, and cultural heritage.

9. **Regulatory Compliance**: Adherence to laws, regulations, and standards governing mining activities, including environmental regulations, health and safety standards, and community engagement requirements.

10. *Stakeholder Engagement*: The process of involving and consulting with individuals, groups, and organizations affected by or

interested in a project or development, including local communities, government agencies, NGOs, and industry stakeholders.

Appendix B: Maps, Charts, and Diagrams

<u>Geological map of Emalahleni showing coal deposits and mining operations</u>

Diagram illustrating the process of coal formation and deposition

Appendix C: References and Further Reading

1. Department of Mineral Resources (South Africa): Official government website providing information on mining regulations, policies, and statistics. Link

2. Chamber of Mines South Africa: Industry association representing mining companies in South Africa. Link

3. World Coal Association: International organization providing information on coal mining, production, and sustainability. Link

4. Environmental Impact Assessment (EIA) Regulations, 2014: Legislation governing environmental impact assessments for mining projects in South Africa. Link

5. South African Mining Charter: Policy framework aimed at promoting transformation and equity in the mining industry. Link

6. "Mining and Communities: Understanding the Context of Mining and Its Impacts on Communities in South Africa" by Ingrid Watson et al. (2018): A comprehensive study examining the social, economic, and environmental impacts of mining on communities in South Africa. Link

7. "Coal Mining in South Africa: A Review of Current Practices and Environmental Impacts" by Vuso Mdluli et al. (2020): A scientific review article discussing the environmental impacts of coal mining in South Africa and potential mitigation strategies. Link

These references provide valuable insights and resources for readers interested in exploring the topic of mining in Emalahleni in more detail.

Don't miss out!

Visit the website below and you can sign up to receive emails whenever Hemilton Thabo Mtsweni publishes a new book. There's no charge and no obligation.

https://books2read.com/r/B-A-GWJFB-AFYZC

BOOKS2READ

Connecting independent readers to independent writers.

About the Author

Author Profile: HT Mtsweni

Biographical Information:HT Mtsweni is a prolific and esteemed author affiliated with HTN Publishers, a subsidiary of HTN Nsimbiken Holdings. While specific biographical details may vary, Mtsweni's literary contributions have garnered attention for their depth, insight, and captivating storytelling.

HT Mtsweni's literary contributions stand as a testament to the enduring power of storytelling and the profound impact of literature on the human spirit. Through their works, Mtsweni invites readers to embark on transformative journeys of self-discovery, empathy, and understanding.

www.ingramcontent.com/pod-product-compliance
Lightning Source LLC
Chambersburg PA
CBHW020330180726
47991CB00019B/1113